EXCE

For

BEGINNERS

✍ A Step by Step Guide to Learn Excel in One Day ✍

Elite Tech Academy

type of guarantee assurance. While we try to keep the information up-to-date and correct, there are no representations or warranties, express or implied, about the completeness, accuracy, reliability, suitability or availability with respect to the information, products, services, or related graphics contained in this book for any purpose.

The trademarks that are used are without any consent, and the publication of the trademark is without permission or backing by the trademark owner. All trademarks and brands within this book are for clarifying purposes only and are owned by the owners themselves, not affiliated with this document.

The author claims no responsibility to any person or entity for any liability, loss or damage caused or alleged to be caused directly or indirectly as a result of the use, application or interpretation of the information presented herein.

Introduction

*W*elcome to the exciting world of EXCEL! I am so glad that you picked up this book.

Thirty years after it was introduced, Excel remains the most popular business software across America. However, a lot of people are still unable to adequately use it to perform even basic operations.

Excel is one of the most powerful software tools in the world for collecting, analyzing and summarizing data but its incredible power often comes at a cost. Excel is a massive program and it can literally take a beginner months or even years to master it.

Research shows that many first time Excel users don't take advantage of even a small percentage of Excel's complete feature set. Beginners continue to manually enter data instead of easily using formulas and functions that could save them a ton of time and skyrocket their productivity.

My first introduction to Excel was about 15 years ago when I was majoring for my Electrical Engineering degree. At that time, I used it for very basic activities such as keeping account of my course credits and my expenses.

Fast forward to today and I use it almost every day. I use it in my day job to organize data and create reports, Pivot tables and charts. I use these tables and charts to create beautiful presentations to effectively convey my messages. At home, I use it for a variety of tasks including tracking expenses, taxes and schedule planning. Believe it or not, I have even used Excel for my to-do Checklists!

Looking back over the years, I now realize that Excel has been growing and evolving too! Back then, the spreadsheets were not very user friendly and only had basic features. Contrast that with the functions and features available with the latest version of Excel and you will understand how far we have come.

This book is an attempt to document the steps, strategies and information I have learnt over the years that will help you acquire the essentials of Excel in as little time as possible.

It will help you learn some of the most important functions and features of Excel along with some tips and shortcuts. You will become proficient enough to prepare professional reports, format data appropriately, identify trends and create excellent visual presentations.

So let's get started, shall we?

Your FREE EXCEL Resource Guide

$\mathcal{B}$efore we begin, I would like to express my heartfelt gratitude. I know that your time is limited. I also realize that there are many other books and courses about this topic.

You chose to read mine. That means a lot to me!

As a token of appreciation, I would like to give you something. It won't cost you a dime. It's a 40 page Excel resource guide that you could use for your reference.

Please download your FREE guide at the below link

http://amazinglifeforever.com/Gift/excel_resource_guide/

Other Books you Might Like

*I*f you are interested in learning Python, please do check out

PYTHON For Beginners: A Smarter and Faster Way to Learn Python

https://www.amazon.com/dp/B07CWQ4DQ5

"There's an entire flight simulator hidden in every copy of Microsoft Excel 97"

- Bruce Schneier

TABLE OF CONTENTS

Introduction

Your FREE EXCEL Resource Guide

Chapter 1

✒ EXCEL? What EXCEL? ✒

*E*xcel is the most popular spreadsheet software in the world today. It was developed by the giant software company Microsoft Inc. and is the single most widely used spreadsheet program in businesses, government, schools, universities and other institutions.

While there are many different spreadsheet programs available, Excel remains number one. It has continued to enjoy widespread use and massive growth over the past three decades. There have been numerous upgrades and new features introduced over the years.

Excel finds application in many different fields including business intelligence, finance, statistics, analysis, forecasting, billing, inventory, data management, and so much more. This is why numerous employees and workers are required to learn how to use this application if they are to be effective in the workplace.

Most employers view Excel as an essential end-user computing tool, especially those in the fields of accounting, information systems, and business in general. It is widely used to carryout daily functions at the workplace.

✎ What can you do with Excel? ✎

Compile Data Effectively

You can effectively use Excel to compile data and process information from different documents and files and keep them at a single location.

You can also export and import numerical data, text, and images from other spreadsheets to one location.

Access files online

It is quite easy to access Excel files online from varied locations. Excel can be accessed online via Microsoft's Office 365 productivity suite.

Any person, whether an employee or business leader, can access Excel files using any connected device regardless of their location around the world. This provides you an exciting opportunity to work remotely anytime you want.

Identifying Trends

Data analysis on Excel can help you to identify useful trends in business, commerce, and the financial markets.

When you present information and data in the form of graphs and charts to others, you will be able to include useful features such as the average line. This line can clearly point out important trends that emerge from the data. Such information can help influence policy and decision making in boardrooms.

Business can also use the information to develop future strategies.

Develop excellent visual presentations

You can use the data generated on an Excel worksheet to unlock the potential of a company. When you enter data in an organized manner, then you can apply formulae to sort, filter, add, and manipulate it to provide useful visual presentations.

These include clustered columns, graphs, and pie charts. They can be effectively used by a business to produce reports and also prepare effective marketing messages.

Format data effectively

When using Excel, you can format the spreadsheet and the data on it using various options such as italics, bold fonts, and different colors and so on, to single out and differentiate between columns and sections of pie charts. This way, it is possible to make useful data or figures stand out from the rest.

It also makes it easy to compare figures and values, highlight rows, and even compare lists.

Other things that you can achieve with Excel

- You can manipulate text
- Import and store data
- Create graphs and charts
- Crunch and workout numbers
- Automate tasks
- Prepare templates and so much more

Chapter 2

✎ A Brief History of Excel ✎

Spreadsheets can be traced back to the late 1970s with the release of VisiCalc on the Apple II computer. It is this application that took the PC computer from the hands of gamers and academics and into the business world.

A couple of years later, Microsoft, hot on the heels of Apple, released a similar software program known as Multiplan. Lotus 123, released in 1983, dealt a death blow to all previous spreadsheet programs. Lotus 123 was superior to all the others, especially its database and charting functions.

However, in 1985, Microsoft launched MS Excel 1 on the Apple computer. It was essentially the first spreadsheet software to be controlled by using a mouse.

At its release, Excel was meant to achieve everything that Lotus 123 did but much faster and better. By 1989, Excel was the dominant spreadsheet program, and Lotus 123 eventually became obsolete.

Excel Versions

There have been a number of Excel versions released over the years. ·

They include Excel 3 released in 1990, Excel 4 released in 1992, Excel 5 in 1993 and Excel 7 in 1995.

Excel 97 – 2003

In 1997, Microsoft released Excel 8 which was also known as Excel 97. By the time Microsoft released Excel 2000, it was already integrated into Microsoft Office 2000. This is an entire package of programs that was released in 2000.

Excel 2000 contained advanced features such as IRM Tools, List Ranges, and Smart Tags. It includes some upgrades and a feature that supports XML which allows data to be imported from other applications.

Excel 2007 – 2013

The 2007 Excel version moved to the beneficial albeit radical Ribbon interface. The workbooks were significantly improved so they could store more data and could handle 16000 columns and up to 1 million rows.

Excel 2010 is a lot like its 2007 predecessor with only subtle improvements. Some of the main changes included easier access to table and chart commands, an improved ribbon, and better usability.

Excel 2016 – to date

This is the latest and current Excel version available. It comes with major database enhancements, quick data analysis tools, new charts and plenty of other features.

You also get access to 3-D power maps, new templates as well as ease of sharing and collaboration. All these new and improved features make Excel one of the most versatile, essential, and must-have software programs for the modern workplace.

Chapter 3

❧ Basic EXCEL Terminology ❧

You can think of MS Excel as a spreadsheet consisting of rows and columns that constitute a table. If you open up an Excel workbook, you will observe letters running across from left to right aligned to columns while the rows have numbers.

In Excel terminology, any point where a row meets a column is referred to as a "cell".

Let's go over the most essential Excel terms that you will need to get familiar with.

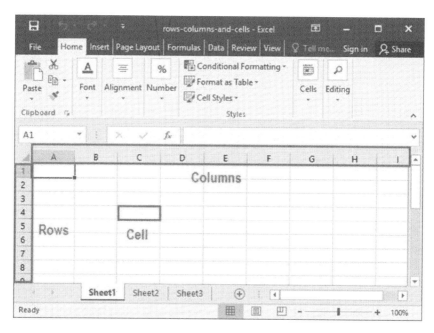

Image courtesy of deskbrite.com

Rows and Columns

Excel consists of blocks of cells on a spreadsheet.

These cells are arranged in rows running horizontally across while columns run vertically.

Cell

A cell can be defined as a single block or rectangle found in a worksheet. It is the basic unit that contains data.

The data can be a number, text, results of calculations and so on. A cell that is open for editing is referred to as an active cell.

Merged Cell

A merged cell is a cell that results after two or more cells are combined into one single cell.

Workbook

A workbook is an Excel file or spreadsheet. It contains all the data entered and allows you to manipulate, alter, delete, sort, and even calculate results.

The default name of any workbook in Excel is *Book 1*. It will be saved under this name if not changed.

You can think of a workbook as an accounting ledger book where individual pages are the worksheets.

Worksheet

A worksheet is a spreadsheet found in an Excel workbook.

A workbook can have one or more worksheets nestled in it. You will find worksheets at the bottom left-hand side of a workbook in the form of tabs.

An active worksheet is one that you are currently working on.

Ribbon

Towards the top portion of a workbook, you will find a row of buttons and command tabs which is referred to as a Ribbon.

The Ribbon actually takes the place of toolbars and menus that were present in earlier Excel versions. Each tab on the Ribbon comes with numerous options.

Some of the tabs include Insert, Page Layout, and Home. When you click on each tab, you will see all the options under that particular tab.

Array

The term Array refers to a number of cells that are grouped together. An array could be, for example, C6: C16.

This informs any formula you use to read data from cell C6 to cell number C16.

Cell Range

A collection of cells jointly identified as a group is also known as a cell range. These cells are often defined using certain criteria.

The range, also known as an array, can easily be determined on Excel. As an example, you can have a cell range from B2:D7.

If a formula is to be used, then the range will inform the bounds of the formula. Sometimes a range can exceed beyond a single worksheet within the same workbook.

Cell Reference

Any set of coordinates that identify an individual cell constitute a cell reference. This reference includes both letters and numbers.

C4, for instance, refers to a cell found along the C column and row number 4.

Cell Formatting

The term cell formatting refers to the process of changing the way data is displayed on a spreadsheet.

Any time a cell is formatted, the information is displayed

differently, but the cell's content remains unchanged.

Name Box

The name of a table, cell, or range of cells is always displayed in the Name Box.

A range of cells and even individual cells can be named using the Name Box. But worksheets can only have one name.

AutoSum

When you use this feature, it will simply sum up all entries and provide you with the result in a cell of your choosing.

AutoFill

This feature allows you to easily copy data onto a number of different cells.

Source Data

Source data is a term that refers to any information that you used to create a Pivot Table field to rearrange the display of a report.

Pivot Table

The Pivot Table is a useful data summarization tool. It is mainly applied in situations where data needs to be automatically summed up.

Data is first obtained through one table then displayed on another table.

Formula Bar

The contents of an active cell are often displayed on what is known as a Formula Bar.

Excel makes wide use of formulas which enable to perform automated calculations within a worksheet and even across workbooks.

Formulas must be typed starting with a = sign. There are plenty of different formulas that you can use as well as all the basic arithmetic operators such as add, subtract, multiply, and even divide.

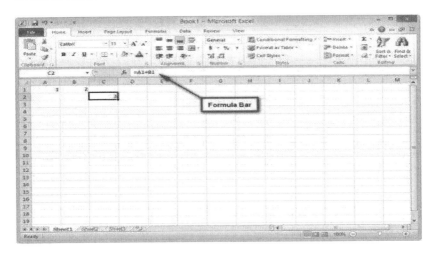

Formula Bar, Courtesy of www.turbofuture.com

Template

A formatted workbook that is purposely prepared to enable users to achieve a particular purpose is known as a template.

For instance, calendars and payment invoices are all examples of an Excel template.

Operator

Signs and symbols that show you which calculation is essential in an expression are known as operators. However, they are not necessarily mathematical only.

They can also include reference, comparison, and even text operators.

Error Code

Basically, an error code will be seen anytime Excel encounters a problem within a given formula.

There are lots of Excel terms out there. The few that we have mentioned above can help you get started on your journey to master this useful application.

Chapter 4

The EXCEL User Interface

*E*xcel 2016 comes with a pretty compact user interface with plenty of different features.

It is important that you familiarize yourself with this interface because it will enable you to maximize its potential.

The Worksheet

Worksheets are the main working area of an Excel workbook. They appear in the form of tabs at the bottom left side of the Excel workbook window.

Each workbook can potentially have an infinite number of worksheets.

Worksheets consist primarily of cells which are prominently displayed in the form of a grid.

Cells are a result of intersection between rows and columns. At the far right of the worksheet are scroll bars. These come in handy when you want to scroll up and down the worksheet.

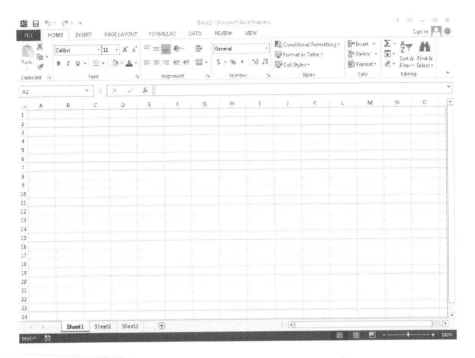

Excel User Interface – Image courtesy of excel2013.info

Toolbar

On the top left-hand corner, there is the Quick Access Toolbar. It can be found just above the Ribbon.

You can very easily customize this toolbar by adding any commands you deem essential or useful.

The Quick Access Toolbar enables you easily access all the useful commands. These include commands such as Repeat, Undo, and Save.

Ribbon

Excel 2013 has a tabbed Ribbon in place of the old menu. It comes with a number of tabs each containing several commands.

Using the tabs, you will be able to accomplish some of the simplest and common tasks in Excel.

The ribbon can be minimized when not readily needed and then maximized for easy access whenever the need arises. It is designed to be responsive to your immediate tasks, but you have the liberty to minimize if you think it takes up too much space.

Backstage View

The Backstage View provides you with easy choices to open, save, print, and share any of your Excel workbooks. Accessing this function is pretty easy.

Simply click on the file tab on the Excel Ribbon.

✎ Excel Themes & Templates ✎

*I*f you are using any Excel version from 2007 and beyond,

then you can select one out of hundreds of different themes and templates.

Excel has numerous theme-enabled templates which you can use with your workbooks. These come in a variety of graphic design, effects, fonts, and colors.

If you want to find a great template for your workbook, all you need to do is proceed to the Page Layout and choose themes.

Now place your mouse over the different themes, and you will view a slick display of some of the most impressive ones.

Sometimes you want an entire new theme for your workbook. At other times, you may prefer to only have some changes but not take up an entire theme.

If, for instance, you do not want to alter your theme in totality, which means fonts and colors as well, then just select your preferred from an entire gallery of colors.

However, you cannot choose different theme colors for your template if you are using Excel versions that existed before 2007. This is because the templates designed prior to 2007 did not use the current theme fonts and color palette.

✍ Theme-Enabled Excel Templates ✍

If you want to find suitable themes, you can browse through official MS Office themes on your Excel workbook or on different sites online. Some of the best theme-enabled templates are designed with users in mind.

For instance, they come with all the essential features that are inherent in all latest Excel models. They also come with conditional formatting, tables and other features found in the latest Excel models.

You can find invoice templates, receipt templates, accounting templates, balance sheets and so many more. They come in different designs, varying colors, and so much more.

All you have to do is browse through the catalog and simply choose a template that you like. Even then, studies indicate that most people prefer to print their documents in black and white, and sometimes in a professionally looking dark blue.

Color documents often turn out poorly if you do not have a color printer so be wary about that.

With a theme enabled template, you can easily switch between colored or black and white printing. This way, you can easily decide whether to print your templates in color or black and white.

✒ Excel Table Designs ✒

There are new types of data tables for Excel. These are presented as data that is beautifully and neatly arranged in columns and rows.

The data table also comes with a footer row with all the totals and the header row.

Excel allows you to choose among a wide variety of different tables. They come in different colors, themes, and designs.

They are best for presenting different kinds of data from numerical to alpha-numerical. However, you should select your tables carefully so that your formulas and other important details are preserved even if you manipulated data or made changes to the cell.

Ideally, this is what you need to be on the lookout for.

- You should be able to easily copy and paste rows without affecting the columns and also insert data without upsetting the outcome.

- Try and ensure for the most part that any new row inserted into the table will automatically copy the pre-existing formula.

Sometimes some tables are not compatible with the latest versions or some versions of Excel. Therefore, be sure to confirm which ones are compatible before choosing one.

The great part is that modern templates and tables are compatible with the latest versions of Excel. You also get to enjoy conditional formatting, pretty graphs, sparkling tables, custom formats and so much more.

Excel tables and templates can find practical use in things such as Timesheets, budget planners, home inventory and annual calendars.

Chapter 5

ᓚGetting Started with EXCEL ᓚ

*H*ow to Open a New Excel File

Opening a new Excel workbook is a very easy process. An Excel File is simply a workbook that consists of one or more worksheets. These worksheets can be used to organize any data and present any information that you want.

Here is the process of opening a new Excel file.

First, launch Excel and ensure that it is active and running on your computer.

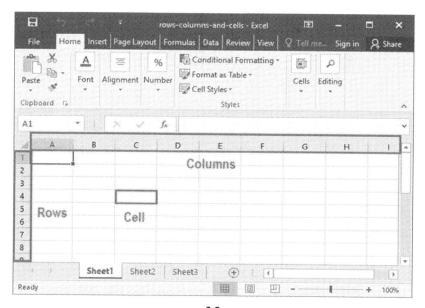

Go to the top left of Excel and click on *File* then choose *New* from the menu.

You will then select to open a new *Blank Workbook* under the options. You can also easily open a new workbook by pressing CTRL + N.

The new workbook will be live, and you can start editing, adding, and summing up data within a short period of time.

While the new File gives you only one worksheet, you can easily increase these to suit your needs.

✍ How to Navigate Excel Cells ✍

There are multiple ways of navigating through the cells. These ways include jumping between cells and highlighting a whole range of cells.

One of the easiest ways of doing this is to click on a cell with your mouse.

Clicking on an individual cell identifies it and enables you to enter data, delete or otherwise work with it.

You can also highlight a number of cells. All you need to do is click on a single cell and drag it along the area you want to be highlighted.

The problem arises if you have a very large spreadsheet as this could be tedious and take plenty of your time. Fortunately, there are a number of tips and shortcuts that you could use to make things easier, faster and more effective.

The SHIFT and CONTROL keys are some of the most important keys that you should get familiar with.

SHIFT Key

When you click on a particular cell and then hold the Shift key down, all the items next to that cell will be highlighted.

If you then click the arrow to the left, then all items to the left of that cell will be highlighted. If on the other hand, you click on the down arrow, then the entire area below the cell will be highlighted.

Also, if you click on a cell, hold down the Shift key and then click on another cell, then all the cells in between the two will all be highlighted.

CONTROL Key

This is also another very useful key. For instance, if you click on a cell, then press and hold the control key, then you can use the down key to highlight all cells with data and stop just before an empty cell.

✎ Excel Tabs ✎

Tabs are sometimes referred to as Worksheets. You can add more tabs when using Excel. Tabs enable you to separate your data while ensuring it is easily accessible.

When you open Excel on your computer, it starts you off with only a single sheet. However, you can add more sheets to the workbook.

Worksheet tabs

The worksheet tabs are located at the bottom left-hand side of the worksheet. Tabs are used for purposes of displaying the worksheet.

You can easily navigate through different worksheets by clicking on the relevant tab. For instance, you can click on the tab marked "Sheet 1" to view and work on worksheet 1.

Each Excel workbook can have more than one worksheet even though the default number is three. The tabs are usually labeled as "Sheet 1", "Sheet 2", and "Sheet 3".

If your workbook or file contains the standard number of worksheets, but you desire more, then it is possible to add some more tabs.

Here is the Procedure

1. First, open your Excel workbook. You can do this from your

computer's "Start" menu. Then choose from here which workbook you would love to open.

2. Now, navigate to the bottom left side of your chosen workbook, and you will see the tabs. At the end of the tab series, you will notice a "+" sign. Simply click on this symbol, and you will create a new, blank sheet which will be visible next to the original three.

3. You can also create a copy of an existing worksheet if you want to. All you need to do is have a target destination. Simply get to the source worksheet and then use control + C to copy the contents and transfer these onto the target worksheet.

4. You can also easily rename a tab or worksheet if you want. All you need to do is to double-click on a tab, and you will then be able to rename it. Additionally, you can alter the tab color by right-clicking on a tab and then choosing the option Tab Color. You will see a wide variety of colors so simply choose your preferred one.

5. Excel also allows you to change the number of default tabs. Simply click on the Office button or File tab and choose options. Find the Popular tab and choose "When creating new workbooks" Under this option, you can change the number of tabs to any number you want.

6. Finally, you can re-arrange the worksheets or re-order them as you want. Simply click on any tab and then drag it to the left or right depending on where you want to locate it.

✒ Useful Tips When Working with Multiple Excel Worksheets ✒

If you are a beginner, then you understand that working with Excel can be a slight challenge even with just one worksheet.

However, when operating more than one worksheet, then the difficulty level increases dramatically especially when dealing with data across worksheets. However, with a few tips and instructions, you can make the process easier and more efficient.

1. How to view multiple worksheets simultaneously

You should first customize your view.

It is often quite confusing when you are working on multiple worksheets and are unsure which one you are working on. This happens often when dealing with multiple worksheets.

- First, open your Excel workbook
- Next click on "New Window" for each worksheet that you wish to have on the workbook
- Go to each window then click on a tab that you wish to view
- As soon as the worksheets are displayed, choose Arrange All button and click
- You will be presented with different arrangement views
- Simply check all windows of the active workbook option

Once you can set this view up, you will enjoy an excellent view of all the worksheets that you need within your workbook.

2. Grouping Worksheets Together

When using Excel workbooks, it is possible to group your worksheets together.

It is much easier and more convenient to format and apply formulas across worksheets that have similar formatting.

Take for instance you wish to alter your bills and rental charges. It would be easier for you if you grouped your monthly bills together so that you enter data only once and it will reflect in all subsequent bills.

- First, go to the worksheet tabs that you wish to edit
- Now click + Shift for worksheets that are adjacent or Click + CTRL for those that are not adjacent. These will then be grouped together

Now simply modify or edit data as you desire then press "Enter."

You can always reverse this process anytime you wish. All that you need to do is to right click and then select the "Ungroup Sheets" option. This is an extremely useful option to have so do not undermine it.

3. How to Link Worksheets using Formulas

It is possible, and actually easy, to relate, manipulate, and use formula between different worksheets. In fact, this can be done rather efficiently.

41

If you want to add the cell values from different worksheets, you can easily create a formula that can achieve this. A simple arithmetic formula that can access data from relevant worksheets will ensure that the necessary values are formulated and formatted as required.

4. Copy Formulas between Different Worksheets

If you repetitively use formulas on your worksheets, then you can copy these formulas to help save time and have a more efficient process.

This is especially useful when you are dealing with data from different worksheets.

- First get to the worksheet where the relevant formula is found
- Then press CTRL + click on the target tab where the formula is to be copied
- Now get to the cell where this formula needs to be copied
- Activate this cell by pressing F2 then press Enter

The formula will then be entered, and the same will be repeated where needed.

Chapter 6

ᐯ Excel Formulas & Functions ᐯ

When working with Excel, you need not spend any time doing things manually. Excel has plenty of formulas and functions that you can make use of to achieve your goals.

By using these formulas, you will decrease the amount of time you spend organizing your affairs. It will also ensure that your reports are accurate and more reliable.

Just to clarify, a **Formula** is an expression that calculates the value of a cell. **Functions** are predefined formulas and are already available in Excel.

All formulas must be preceded by a "=" sign and followed by the name of the function. This will be followed by a set of brackets to include any arguments for that function.

Before we go into further details regarding formulas and functions, I think it's very important for you to understand about cell references.

There are essentially two types of cell references in Excel. These are **relative** and **absolute.** They behave differently depending on how and when they are copied and filled into other cells.

Relative references will change relative to wherever the

formula is copied to. All cell references, by default, are relative references hence you would probably be using these the most.

Let's go over a quick example for relative references.

In your excel worksheet, let's have A1 as 20 and B1 as 10 and C1 as =SUM(A1:B1) (C1 cell would be the addition of A1 and B1). Once the function executes, C1 will have the value of 30.

Now, copy over the same function from C1 and paste into C2 cell. You will notice that the formula for the function has now changed to =SUM(A2:B2). If you execute this function, C2 will have the value of 0! This is because the cells A2 and B2 currently do not have any values hence excel defaults these to 0.

I hope you now get an idea of how relative references work.

There may be instances where you would want the cell references to be exactly the same when you copy it to different cells. In these cases, you could use Absolute references. These will remain constant no matter where they are copied.

For an absolute reference, you would need to insert a dollar ($) sign preceding the column reference, or row reference, or both, depending on which reference you would prefer to remain constant.

Here are the typical usages of absolute references

$A1 – When copied, the column reference will not change while the row reference will change

A$1 – When copied, the row reference will not change while the column reference will change

$A$1 – When copied, the row and column references will not change

In our previous example, if you would prefer that the reference values used in the formula for C1 would remain the same when copied over to C2 cell, then the formula for C1 would need to change to

=SUM ($A$1:$B$1)

Once the above function executes, C1 will still have a value of 30 whereas the value for C2 cell will now match C1 (30). This is because the formula in C2 is now referencing the values in A1 and B1 cells.

I would recommend that if you have a pre-existing formula referencing some cells and you would like to copy it directly to a different cell, you should decide **before** copying it over whether you would want any cell references included in the formula to be relative or absolute.

Shortcut Method

Here is a trick I have learnt over the years that will help you to decide quickly between Relative and Absolute references.

Press the F4 Key after you have typed in your cell reference and let Excel do its magic!

In our previous example, the way this would work is that when you are done typing in the formula for the C1 cell

=SUM(A:B)

Press the F4 Key now and Excel will show you the different

45

reference options you could decide to use

(Note: you would need to keep pressing the F4 key to see each different option).

Now that we have covered cell references, let's get back to Formulas and Functions and go over some of the most commonly used Excel functions:

⤚ SUM ⤛

The syntax for this function is as below:

SUM(number1,[number2],...)

The first argument in the above function i.e. number1 is a required argument and refers to the first number that you would like to add. This means that any formula using SUM must have a minimum of 1 number which references one or more cells.

The second and following arguments are optional. The second argument represents the second number you would like to add. In this way, you could specify up to 255 numbers.

Using SUM for calculations

I have been using Excel as my calculator for several years now!

Believe it or not, once you get used to using SUM and other similar mathematical/statistical functions, you would never want to go back to using a traditional calculator since Excel is so intuitive and straightforward.

If you would like to add the values in cells A5 through A10, then the formula would be

=SUM(A5:A10)

If you would like the result of this addition to be multiplied by 3, then the formula would look like

=SUM(A5:A10)*3

Similarly, if you need the result to be divided by 10, then the formula would look like

=SUM(A5:A10)/10

I hope you can see how easy this is but this is just the beginning!

There are many other ways to use this function.

Here are a few of those ways

QUICKSUM

If you are in a hurry, then you could select the range of cells and then use the Status Bar (at the lower right hand side of your Excel workbook) to quickly get the sum of a range of cells.

Values
$89.28
$34.21
$73.53
$2.27
$55.98
$99.67
$43.29
$10.56

Average: $51.10   Count: 8   Sum: $408.78

Image courtesy of support.office.com

In our previous example, if you select cells A1 and B1 and look at the status bar, you would see the below

AVERAGE: 15   COUNT: 2   SUM: 30

As you can see, the status bar also computes the AVERAGE and the COUNT along with the SUM

AUTOSUM

You could also use the AUTOSUM wizard to execute this function.

Going back to our previous example where we have A1 as 20 and B1 as 10, if you select the C1 cell and then go to the ribbon at the top of the worksheet and select FORMULAS->AUTOSUM->SUM, Excel will insert the below formula into

C1

=SUM(A1:B1)

Please do note that this method will only work on contiguous ranges

In addition to SUM, the AutoSum wizard can also help with the many other functions. A few are listed below

AVERAGE (this function will return the average of the arguments provided)

MIN (this function will return the smallest number in a set of values provided)

MAX (this function will return the largest number in a set of values provided)

Count numbers (this function will count the number of cells that contain numbers)

In addition to the above methods, SUM can also be used with other Functions.

⚞COUNT⚟

The syntax for the COUNT function is as below

=COUNT(value1, [value2],...)

The first argument for this function i.e. value1 is a required argument and refers to the first item, reference or range within which the numbers need to be counted.

The second and following arguments are optional. The second argument represents the second item, cell reference or range that you would like to add.

The function that this formula performs is simply to count the number of cells within a given range.

It will search for cells that contain a value in them, so it works only with cells that contain numbers.

Let's use the below example to demonstrate the usage of this function

In your worksheet, please type in the below values in cells A1 through A4

33.44

2

12/8/2018

String

In cell B1, we will use the COUNT Function as follows

=COUNT (A1:A4)

Once the function executes, you will find that the value in cell B1 is 3. The function essentially looked at the values in all 4 cells and ignored the one that was not a number (in this case, value in cell A4 is not a number)

✎ COUNTA ✎

The COUNTA function is very similar to the COUNT function except that COUNTA counts the number of cells that are not empty in a range

This function takes into consideration all cells within the selected range that contain a value or characters. It is suitable for all data types because it looks at all non-empty cells regardless of the data contained.

If we use COUNTA for our previous example

=COUNTA(A1:A4)

the value of B1 would be 4. This is because COUNTA is only looking for the number of cells that are non-empty.

✎ LEN and LENB ✎

The syntax for the LEN and LENB functions are as below

LEN(text)

LENB(text)

Where text is a required argument and represents the text whose length you want to find. Please do note that spaces do count as characters in these functions.

The LEN function can be used to find out the total no of characters in a text.

The LENB function will return the number of bytes used to represent the characters in a text.

⚡LEFT, MID, RIGHT ⚡

The functions LEFT (character, text, number), RIGHT (character, text, numeral) and MID (text, character, start number) basically workout and report the total number of characters that are contained within a string of characters.

The syntax for these functions is as below:

LEFT(text, num_chars)

Where text is a required argument and contain the characters that need to be extracted.

num_chars is an optional argument and refers to the number of characters that LEFT is expected to extract from the text.

MID(text, start_num, num_chars)

Where text is a required argument and contain the characters that need to be extracted.

Start_num is a required argument and refers to the position of the first character that needs to be extracted from the text.

num_chars is a required argument and refers to the number

of characters that MID is expected to extract from the text.

RIGHT(text, [num_chars])

Where text is a required argument and contain the characters that need to be extracted.

num_chars is an optional argument and refers to the number of characters that RIGHT is expected to extract from the text

Please do keep the below rules in mind regarding the [num_chars] argument while using these functions:

1) The default value of [num_chars] is 1. So if this argument is not specified in the formula, it is assumed to be 1
2) The functions will return all the text if [num_chars] is greater than the length of the text
3) [num_chars] must always be greater than or equal to 0

The RIGHT function returns the last character or characters in a text, based on the number of characters specified

The MID function returns a specific number of characters from a text, starting at the position specified and based on the number of characters specified.

The LEFT function returns the first character or characters in a text, based on the number of characters specified.

When using the MID function, you will need to specify where

you want it to begin the count.

Using these three functions can help you determine the content of a cell if it contains a string of characters.

TRIM

TRIM (C4) is a function that helps you to get rid of all spaces from a text within a particular cell. This, however, excludes the single spaces between words.

There are many instances when data, retrieved from databases often contains unnecessary spaces for no good reason. It can be difficult handling or manipulating such data.

Fortunately, the TRIM function can help you eliminate the spaces.

The syntax for this function is as below:

TRIM(text)

where text is a required argument and specifies the text from which spaces need to be removed

VLOOKUP

VLOOKUP is one of the most popular functions used in Excel and is the most widely used.

What it does is search for a value at the left column within a table and then provides a value within the same row that you have specified.

What happens here is that you simply get to define a Look Value and the function will search for it. This value will be searched within the leftmost column within the table.

To get an accurate result, ensure that you provide a numeral or number for the Lookup Value.

Now the function will proceed to look for the relevant data, and if a match is found, then the value will be returned and the index used is "index_num".

Always endeavor to copy-paste the entire formula within all the cells in the specified column. This ensures that you receive a properly aligned list with all the relevant figures and essential data.

This function, just like many others, finds practical application in commerce, business, banking, and even the modern workplace.

The syntax for this function is as below

=VLOOKUP (value, table, col_index, [range_lookup])

Where "value" refers to the value you want to look up in a table. This value should be present in the first column of the table

"table" refers to the table from which you want to retrieve a value

"col_index" refers to the column in the table from which to

retrieve a value

"[range_lookup]" is an optional argument and can be either 1/TRUE or 0/FALSE. If you specify [range_lookup] as TRUE, then you are looking for an approximate match whereas FALSE refers to an exact match. This argument is TRUE by default.

Let's use the below example to demonstrate the usage of this function

In your excel worksheet, please type in the below state names in cells A1 through A4

California

Texas

Arizona

Colorado

Please type in the below state capitals in cells B1 through B4

Sacramento

Austin

Phoenix

Denver

Now, let's use the VLOOKUP function to find out the state capital for Arizona

Please type in the below formula in cell C1

VLOOKUP(A3, A1:B4, 2, FALSE)

A3 cell refers to Arizona (since we are trying to look up the value of Arizona state

A1:B4 refers to the complete table that extends from A1 through B4 cells (you could also specify this as $A$1:$B$4 – going back to our discussion regarding cell references at the beginning of this chapter)

2 refers to the column from which we would like the function to retrieve the value (since we know that the text Phoenix is in the 2nd column i.e B)

And finally, [range_lookup] is FALSE since we are looking for an exact match

Once the above function executes, the value of C1 cell should be

Phoenix

IF Statements

Whenever you are performing any analysis on data, then you are likely to encounter plenty of different scenarios.

Data may have to respond differently to each of these

scenarios, and this is where the IF statements come in handy.

IF (logical statement, return a certain result if statement is true, otherwise return this if logical statement not true).

Anytime you undertake an analysis of data then you are likely to see different scenarios depending on circumstances. It is easy to demonstrate this with an example.

Consider a salesman with a certain quota that he has to meet. The salesman can use an IF statement to indicate whether the quota was met or not.

(IF salesperson meets quota, then say "Quota met" otherwise if the quota is not met, then say "Quota not met.")

It is much easier if the statement is said out loud in this manner rather than use more complicated methods that not everyone can follow.

It would also make it easier to use NESTED IF statements for the same issue. It is much better when the IF statement shows the outcome rather than having to figure things out manually.

CONCATENATE

The term CONCATENATE simply refers to the process of combining data in different cells into a single cell. There is an Excel function that can help you achieve this feat.

The syntax for this function is as below

CONCATENATE(text1, [text2], ...)

Where text1 is a required argument and specifies the first item that needs to be joined. This item could be a text, number or a cell reference.

Text2 and other successive arguments are optional and specify the additional items that need to be joined.

Let us use an example to demonstrate this.

In your worksheet, please type in "Sir" (without the double quotes) in Cell A1 and "Newton" in cell B1

In Cell C1, please type in the below formula

=CONCATENATE(A1," ", B1)

Once the above function executes, the text in C1 cell would be

Sir Newton

The quotation marks in the formula above simply include a space between the two text items.

COUNTIF, SUMIF, AVERAGEIF

These are very important Excel functions. They perform their respective functions should a certain condition be met.

The formulas are as follows;

=SUMIF(criteria, range, sum_range),

=AVERAGEIF(criteria, average_range, range) and

=COUNTIF(range, criteria)

These functions not only perform their core criteria such as calculate sum and average but also any additional IF condition you provide. Therefore, when you come up with a formula, you should include all the appropriate conditions.

Excel Formulas and Functions

There are more than 316 formulas and functions in Excel. It is not possible to learn about all of them and know instantly which one to use. That is quite a challenge.

Fortunately, Excel provides an easy-to-use method that helps you identify the specific formula you wish to use. There is an inbuilt wizard that can help you find the function that you need to use.

Simply Click on "*fx*" that is located next to the Excel formula bar (just above the column indicators A, B....). Clicking on the "*fx*" button reveals a menu which allows you to describe the kind of help you need.

When you enter what you need, the wizard will try to identify the correct function that you need to use.

For instance, if you need to eliminate any extra spaces, then the wizard will suggest you use the TRIM function.

There are many other functions including ABD, OR, TODAY, DAY, and so many others. Combining these functions provides you with the real power that you need to solve complex problems and challenges.

For the complete list of all Functions, please download the EXCEL resource guide if you haven't already

http://amazinglifeforever.com/Gift/excel_re source_guide/

Chapter 7

⌐ Worksheet Formatting & Presentation ⌐

*I*mporting Data into Excel from Different Sources

1. Importing data from My SQL Server

You can easily import data into your Excel workbook from an SQL Server.

SQL has an Import and Export wizard that lets you easily transfer data from both sources. This makes it very easy to copy data from one source to another.

You get to select the destination file and the exact amount or type of data you wish to transfer. This is all achieved through what is known as an SSIS package or SQL Server Integration Services package.

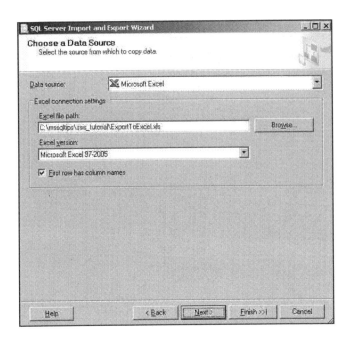

Photo courtesy of mssqltips.com

Process

1. First, open the SQL server wizard from the "Start" menu. Also, you could start it from the SQL Server Management Studio.

2. Once it is opened, find the database that is the source of the data you wish to import. Simply right-click on the database and then choose Import Data which is an option that is provided on the menu

3. Now connect the server to the Excel workbook via the wizard.

4. MS Excel can be selected as the destination of the data.

5. The wizard facilitates the connectivity between source and destination

6. You can choose a particular database on Excel where the data will be stored

7. Click "Next" and then "Finish" to complete the process

Now just wait for a second or two until the server confirms that the action has taken place. These few yet simple steps provide an easy guide on how to import data from an SQL database into an Excel database.

The process can be reversed and data copied from an Excel database directly to an SQL Server or any other destination.

⟡ Hiding Rows & Columns in Excel ⟡

Did you know that hiding rows and columns in Excel is not only possible but also very easy as well? There are actually several ways of achieving this.

The best part is that you can also unhide any cells, rows, or columns that you hide. There are tools that you can use to help you hide and unhide cells conveniently.

One such tool is Excel's Grouping Tool.

1. Hide Rows and Columns and then Unhide

First, you need to select the exact rows and columns that you wish to hide. You can easily achieve this using the Control key if you wish to also have non-contiguous columns and rows or those not next to or adjacent to each other.

Now go to the Home button and click "Format" and select "Hide Rows and Columns."

You can also highlight a row or columns and Right Click then choose the Hide option. This simple process will ensure that all the selected rows and columns are hidden.

2. How to Unhide the Rows and Columns

If you wish to reverse the above process, then you can do so easily.

First, go the Home tab and click on the "Format" button. Now from the options on the drop-down menu, find Unhide Columns and Rows and click on it.

You will then unhide all the hidden columns and rows. Alternatively, you can get to the area of interest, highlight the hidden rows and columns, Right click using the mouse the highlighted area and choose Unhide Rows and Columns.

The columns and rows will then be visible again.

⌒ Importing Data from the Web to Excel ⌒

Manual importation of data from a webpage to your Excel

workbook can be tedious, error-prone, and time-consuming. You could easily discover that all the data you copy is pasted into a single cell.

It is much easier to import data to Excel using the "Web query" tool.

This is a tool designed to help you import data much faster, more conveniently, and accurately, saving you plenty of time in the process. This tool can be used to obtain both static and active data from the Internet.

Procedure to Import Data from the Web to Excel

1) Open your Excel workbook then click on "File."
2) Select "Import External Data" then choose "Create New Web Query."
3) Now just copy the web address of the website where you want to obtain data from then paste this address or URL into the address box.

And that is it. Once you enter the URL address, Excel will proceed to import the data for you and organize appropriately into a single page or multiple pages depending on the size and amount of data.

The process is even easier if you are using the Explorer browser. It allows you to import data directly from the web to your excel workbook.

First get to the relevant webpage that contains the information that you need.

Next, proceed to right click on the webpage and after that choose "Export to Microsoft Excel." You will then view a display saying, "New Web Query."

If you ever come across a table containing useful data on the web, simply use the web query tool to import the data onto an Excel page. You can also use the same process to import live data as it is generated.

⚞ Fixing Data in Excel ⚟

Sometimes data gets messed up either during importation or even when entering.

When this happens, values that seem like numbers appear as a string of characters to Excel. They can therefore not be manipulated or processed arithmetically.

Fortunately, such errors can be fixed.

For instance, when you copy numbers directly from a webpage or any other source, it may be received as text. Some values may look like numbers to the eye but are recognized as text by Excel.

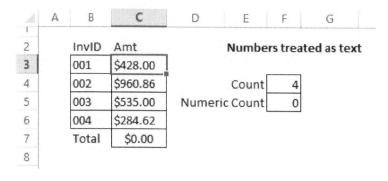

	InvID	Amt		Numbers treated as text	
	001	$428.00			
	002	$960.86		Count	4
	003	$535.00		Numeric Count	0
	004	$284.62			
	Total	$0.00			

Data that appears as texts courtesy of contextures.com

Fixing problem of Numbers Viewed as Texts

1) First, you should select a set of blank or empty cells where you would want the final fixed data to be pasted.

2) Now choose all the cells with the numbers currently viewed as text or characters

3) Then choose one of the chosen cells and right-click then click "Paste Special"

4) Now a pop-up widow should come up with the title "Paste Special". In this window, please select "Values" in the paste section and "Add" in the Operation section.

5) Then simply click OK and the pop-up window should disappear.

After you click "OK," all the presumed texts will be converted into characters. You will then be able to proceed to format and even manipulate the data and apply any formulas you want.

Using Macros for Regular Text to Number Conversion

For anyone who regularly needs to convert text or characters, it is much easier to create and use a macro.

A macro in computing is a single instruction that is designed to execute a particular task.

First get a macro that has the capacity to convert text to numbers on Excel.

Store this macro in one of the Excel workbooks that you use regularly.

You can include a button in a toolbar and then connect the macro to that particular button.

Once this is done, you will easily be able to fix the problem by simply selecting the affected cells and then clicking that button from the toolbar.

✑ Fixing Any Hidden Characters ✑

You might, on occasion, copy data from a website and then transfer it to your Excel workbook riddled with errors such as hidden characters.

These can include unnecessary commas, special characters,

and even periods.

Any non-breaking space is usually referred to as character 160. This kind of character error cannot be fixed simply by using some digit cleanup techniques.

Sometimes Excel users may attempt a manual search to fixing such problems. However, this can be time-consuming and tedious.

The macro shown below can help fix that. All you need to do is use this macro and attach it to a button on your Excel toolbar.

Now, all that you need to do is simply identify the cells with the hidden characters, select them and simply click on the toolbar button.

```
Sub CleanSelectedRange()
' "Cleans" contents of all selected cells on the active
worksheet
Dim Cell As Range
For Each Cell In Selection
If Not Cell.HasFormula Then
Cell.Value = CleanString(Cell.Value)
End If
Next Cell
End Sub


Function CleanString(StrIn As String, Optional
IsRemoveLineFeeds As Boolean = False) As String

' removes invisible characters, including carriage returns.
By default, LINEFEEDS are NOT removed.
' to REMOVE LINEFEEDS, pass TRUE
' Does not remove special characters like symbols,
international
' characters, etc. This function runs recursively, each
call
' removing one embedded character

  Dim iCh  As Integer
```

```
Dim Ch    As Integer         'a single character to be tested
CleanString = StrIn
For iCh = 1 To Len(StrIn)
  Ch = Asc(Mid(StrIn, iCh, 1))
  If Ch < 32 Then
    ' remove Ch 10 only if option is True
    If (Ch <> 10) Or (Ch = 10 And IsRemoveLineFeeds) Then
      'remove special character
      CleanString = Left(StrIn, iCh - 1) &
CleanString(Mid(StrIn, iCh + 1))
    End If
    Exit Function
  End If
Next iCh

End Function
```

Courtesy of www.mrexcel.com

∼ Convert Currency that has different Separators∼

Sometimes a worksheet may contain data, such as currency, in a format where the separators are different.

For instance, you can have an amount such as GBP 345.20,45 which is converted to US currency as $345,200.45.

Some currencies use the comma as the Decimal separator and the period as the Thousand separator. Other currencies such as the US dollar use the period as its Decimal separator and the comma as the Thousand separator.

Excel has the capacity to fix this anomaly so that both currencies are similarly aligned.

Here is the procedure;

1. First, identify the relevant cells and then highlight them. These are the cells that contain all the relevant numbers.

2. Now Click on "DATA" on the toolbar and then "Text to Columns" within "DATA"

3. A pop up window named "Convert Text to Columns Wizard" should come up. Click on "Next" at the bottom of the window. Click on "Next" a second time and on the resulting screen, please find the "Advanced.." button.

4. Click on the "Advanced.." button and a smaller pop up window named "Advanced Text Import Settings" should come up. You should see 2 separator settings in this window – Decimal separator and Thousands separator.

5. Use the Decimal separator pull down menu and choose the separator currently in use. In our case, we can choose the comma as it is used in both numerals.

6. Use the Thousands separator pull down menu and choose the separator you would like to use. In our case, we can choose the period as our thousands separator for both numerals.

8. Now simply click OK to exit out of the "Advanced Text Import Settings" pop up widow and then finally click on Finish to exit out of the "Convert Text to Columns Wizard" pop up window.

Once you complete the above steps, you should see that both numerals will now have common separators.

To ensure that the data in your spreadsheet is perfect, you need to eliminate all typo errors and other mistakes that arise as you transfer and enter data from various sources.

It is important that you first get Excel to make corrections regarding in data entry errors and typos that may exist. Excel has an Autocorrect feature that enables it to make such corrections.

Also be careful while entering data in making any manual corrections of all errors that you may see. You can do this either after completion of data transfer or during the process.

Autocorrect in Excel

Anyone who uses Excel regularly understands the importance and benefits of using the Autocorrect feature.

It is possible to customize the Autocorrect especially if you are aware of any typos and goofs that you often make.

Autocorrect will save the information you provide it and will then make corrections anytime you make errors and types during data entry.

Autocorrect, when first installed, does some automatic corrections. For instance, it will fix any two capital letters within a word by changing the second capital into a small letter.

Autocorrect also changes all proper nouns such as names of people, days of the week and so on by capitalization.

You are free to add to the list of text and data replacements so that Autocorrect makes the necessary corrections that you feel are necessary.

By customizing this important feature, then your workload will be greatly diminished. You can include correct spellings of words you regularly misspell and so on.

Editing Cells in Excel

Errors are still bound to happen even with Autocorrect.

Correcting these errors and mistakes further will depend more on when you actually notice them.

Ideally, the correction or editing of mistakes will depend on whether you noted these before or after completing the entry.

Here are some suggestions that will help with data editing.

- You can use backspace to delete and correct errors that you note during data entry. Then simply retype the correct entry and move on.

- If you note an error in data entry after completing the cell entry, then you have two options. You can replace the entire cell entry or just edit the errors.

- Replacing the entire entry is a better option for short entries. All you need to do is locate the error and position the mouse pointer next to it. Simply edit the error by deleting the unwanted characters and replacing with the correct ones.

- All you need to do to edit a cell is to double tap or double click on it. This enables you to edit the contents of a particular cell. Now press F2, and you will be able to insert or edit any entries.

Below is a table of keystrokes that can be used in Excel to locate the insertion point within cells. Basically, should you need to enter new characters at the point of insertion, all you need to do is just begin typing and entering data.

If the data is to be deleted and more entered, then switch the insertion key from basic insertion to overtype. This way, old data will be deleted as new data is entered.

Once the data is edited, you will then have to press enter so that the changes are saved and become permanent.

Useful Keystrokes and their Effects

Keystroke	Effect of the Keystroke
Backspace	Deletes data to the left of the insertion point
Left arrow	Positions insertion point to the left of a character
Right arrow	Positions insertion point to the right of a character
Delete	Simply deletes characters to the right of the insertion point
Home	This will move insertion point right at the front of the initial character within a cell
Insert	Enables characters to be entered and can alter from overtype to insert mode

Re-enter the edited contents within the cells so that they are saved by Excel. You can do this by using either the Tab or the Return key.

The arrow keys can also be used to achieve this purpose. They will help in completing this process as required so that all the new data and edited data is correctly entered and edited appropriately.

During the editing mode, the arrow keys will move the cursor within the cell you are editing but no other cells unless you later activate them.

The FREE Excel Resource guide has a complete list of all Excel shortcuts. Here is the link again

http://amazinglifeforever.com/Gift/excel_resource_guide/

Chapter 8

⟆ Intro to Tables in Excel ⟆

What are Tables?

In Excel, a table can be defined as any collection of related columns and rows whose data has to be manipulated separately from other columns and rows within a workbook.

Therefore, once data is separated and converted into a table, it becomes independent of the rest of the content of the worksheet and workbook.

It will acquire its own identity.

Tables are relatively new in Excel. In earlier versions of Excel, they were referred to as lists. Tables were introduced after the 2007 version.

A table is simply a rectangle-shaped dataset that contains data in rows and columns. There are plenty of features that get activated in Excel once a table is created.

✒ Components of an Excel Table ✒

▲	A	B	C	D
1				
2	Product Name ▾	Product Description ▾	Category ▾	Starting Invent
3	Men S Blue	Men Shirt Small Size Blue Color	Men -S	
4	Men S Green	Men Shirt Small Size Green Color	Men -S	
5	Men S Yellow	Men Shirt Small Size Yellow Color	Men -S	
6	Men S Orange	Men Shirt Small Size Orange Color	Men -S	
7	Men S White	Men Shirt Small Size White Color	Men -S	HEADER
8	Men S Red	Men Shirt Small Size Red Color	Men -S	ROW
9	Men M Blue	Men Shirt Medium Size Blue Color	Men -M	
10				
11				

Excel Table with 4 columns – courtesy of indzara.com

Excel tables have what is known as a header row. This is often the top row, and it contains the titles of the columns.

This makes it easy to understand the contents of each column. The columns are sometimes referred to as Fields.

Now if you observe the example table shown above, we have rows and on each row are different products. Each product is unique and hence in its own distinct cell.

Each product has different attributes such as color, size, category, description, and so on. We can enter any type of data in the cells from numerical, alphabetical and even dates and alpha-numeric characters. You can also enter dates and formulas should the need arise.

You can alter the design of the table and choose a design that you like. Using Excel, you can choose from a variety of options such as font types, colors, and even borders. Should you want to change or alter the Table Styles, simply go to the Design Ribbon and check out Table Design.

The best approach when coming up with a table is to use one that clearly indicates the borders of the final row and has clearly marked headers. This way, you or any other person is easily able to view the data within the table. Also, you can better and more clearly see the data in the first row and the last one.

Reading data from one end of the table to the other is easier because of the use of banded rows.

Colored headers help create consistency and also improve the visualization of the data specifically and the table in general. You can choose colors such as blue or green for the headers and red or yellow for entry columns.

Contextual Tabs

After you successfully convert an entire range of data into a table, each table will get its own tab. This tab will appear on the ribbon of your workbook.

Any other table you create within that workbook will also have its own tabs on the ribbon area of your workbook. Such tabs are often referred to as contextual tabs.

These are feature-specific tabs that are available when related features are applied.

Properties of Excel Tables

Name: First, each table has a name. If you do not name your table, then it acquires the name "Table1". The next table you create will be "Table2"and so on. However, if you want to, then you can give each table a specific name.

It is important to name your tables so that it becomes easy to refer to them distinctly and also differentiate it from the other existing tables. Appropriate names will refer to distinct features or purpose of the table. Think of names such as SalesData, ProfitLoss, AccountsData, and so on.

Naming your tables is pretty easy and straightforward. All that you need to do is to go to the Contextual Table then look got the properties group. You will then see the name field where you can enter any name that you want. Remember to use a name that is appropriate to a table and its content for easier reference.

Once the name has been entered, remember to press Enter. This way, the name will change, and the one you entered will become official.

Another way to rename tables in some other Excel versions would be as follows:

1) Highlight the cells that comprise your table in your worksheet.

2) As you highlight the table cells, a "DESIGN" tab will show up in the toolbar.

Image courtesy of PakAccountants.com

3) Click on the "DESIGN" tab and it will open up a whole list of options related to tables.

4) Towards the far left of this newly opened up option bar, you should see an option "Table name:" with a rectangular box at the bottom of this option. If this is your first table for this worksheet and you haven't yet named it, then by default, you would see "Table1" as the name in this box.

5) You can Click within this box and edit the name from "Table1" to whatever name you would prefer. This process will rename your table.

6) The next time you highlight your table cells and click on "DESIGN" tab again, you will observe that the name that shows up in the rectangular box will be the one that you had previously entered.

There are some Table naming rules that you have to observe. One of these is not having any spaces within a name. For instance, you cannot have a name such as "Sales Account" because Excel will return an error message. Therefore, try and ensure you provide one name without any empty spaces in between.

The name can contain numerals but should not start with a number. Also, do not repeat a name that you have already used.

Once you save a table, the name will appear on the Name Box drop-down menu. Of course, you can always change a name that you do not like. This makes accessing any table a quick and convenient process. All that you need to do is to select a table from the name box by just clicking on the name.

Resizing Tables

Excel allows you to alter the size of any tables you have created.

Using the function "Resize Table", you can add or remove columns and rows as you please.

Find the "Resize Table" button (you will find this button just below the "Table Name:" option when you click on the "DESIGN" tab in toolbar) and click on it to adjust the length and height of any table. You can basically choose to have a smaller or larger table depending on your needs.

Also, all selections that you need to make within your table should be made from the top left-hand side of the table. If you do not do this, then Excel will detect this as an error. This is why it is paramount to ensure that such simple rules are observed.

⌒Tools to Use in your Excel Tables ⌒

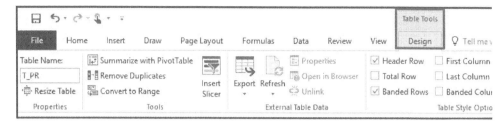

Image courtesy of PakAccountants.com

As mentioned previously, the "Design" tab in the toolbar has many essential options that can help with editing/updating your tables.

Remove Duplicates

Excel allows you to get rid of any duplicate entries within a table. This function is also present in Excel via the Data Tab though having this tab within "DESIGN" is extremely useful.

You can eliminate any duplicate data while ignoring the rest of the entries.

Summarize with Pivot Table

You can summarize the content of your table via the Pivot Table.

The Pivot Table often exists in Excel and can be considered a system Table that provides additional functions such as data analysis.

We will go into a detailed step by step process of using Pivot Tables to create Reports in Chapter 10 "Creating Charts & Reports"

Convert Data to Range

If at any time you feel like you no longer need the table, then you can always convert it back to ordinary data. It is possible to remove the Table and formatted features so that the data is returned to its initial status.

Basically, what you need to do is to deactivate the active Table cells, so the old range of data is reinstated. Please use the "Convert to Range" option for this.

External Table Data

You can share the table and its data on other databases and shared facilities.

Excel allows you to export the Table and its content to computer servers and others where the data may be of use. Please use the "Export" option for this.

⟨Tips and Suggestions ⟩

1) **Always make sure that data is entered directly into the Tables**

A lot of the time, you will find that data was not correctly entered into the tables. This is why Excel users find that the output in the Tables does not reflect the input since the input was incorrectly entered.

Therefore, ensure that the Table Tools ribbon is on to ensure that all the data is entered as required. If the ribbon is not on, then the data was probably not correctly entered, and you should, therefore, check manually and confirm.

You can press CTRL+A to learn the boundaries of the table. Excel will then choose and highlight all the data within the particular cells and then indicate the boundaries.

2. **Remember to use Paste Special as Values when copying and importing data**

Also, whenever you are copying data from a particular source with the intention of pasting them on your worksheet, then always use Paste Special as Values.

If, for instance, you right click inside one of your tables to paste data copied elsewhere, then you will be given the option of Paste Special. Whenever you do, please choose this option and then specify Paste as Values. This way, whatever you paste will be recognized as a value and not as a string of characters.

If you opt for the default copy and paste method, then your

data may not be saved as numerical data but as a string of characters or text.

CTRL+V is not a desirable option when transferring data to a table in Excel. Also, it will paste additional information such as the formulas used and any formatting that was undertaken. Your formulas are likely to be overwritten so be careful each time you have to import data.

3. Always ensure you avoid blank rows

Anytime you enter data, you should ensure there are no rows left blank. Should you notice any blank rows in any table that you are working on, then please proceed to delete them.

They could interfere with any arithmetic, manipulation, or other formulas you intend to use.

4. Ensure that you do not edit any cells that contain formulas

This is also very essential because any formulas you intend to use on your tables are important. They provide a useful function so always ensure that no cells are edited if they contain formulas.

If you edit any such cell by mistake or unknowingly, then simply press CTRL+Z to undo any changes or alterations.

Alternatively, you may find the Resize button and click on it to adjust the length and height of any table. You can basically choose to have a smaller or larger table depending on your needs.

Also, all selections that you need to make within your table should be made from the top left-hand side of the table. If you do not do this, then Excel will detect this as an error.

5. Avoid renaming any fields that contain predefined column labels

Do not rename any of the fields within your table. The reason is that some of the templates used might have made use of pivot tables in calculations and manipulation of figures.

If any change is made, then the calculations used or formulas applied can be changed, altered, or broken.

If, for instance, you right click inside one of your tables to paste data copied elsewhere, then you will be given the option of Paste Special. Whenever you do, please choose this option then specify Paste as Values.

The templates that are readily available to Excel users have custom fields which can easily be renamed without any problems, issues, or concerns.

Custom fields have no problem with formula. You can also add another column or even multiple columns if you wish.

However, always remember not to rename any new fields because this will have an effect on any formulas that you intend to use.

Chapter 9

✑ Creating Charts & Reports ✑

$\mathcal{M}$ost people, especially company executives and business leaders rarely want to spend time reading through pages of reports. It is much easier if they can look at graphs, charts, and reports. Most reports can easily be converted into visual graphs or charts.

It is a fact that relationships and patterns between numbers are better visualized when presented in the form of charts.

You can create and place an Excel chart into a worksheet right next to the relevant data. The chart can also be placed in a different or separate worksheet and even transferred onto other platforms such as MS PowerPoint.

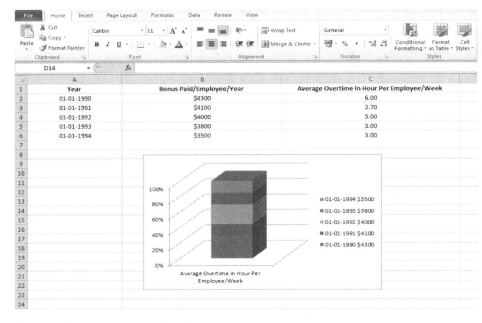

Year	Bonus Paid/Employee/Year	Average Overtime in Hour Per Employee/Week
01-01-1990	$4300	6.00
01-01-1991	$4100	2.70
01-01-1992	$4000	5.00
01-01-1993	$3800	3.00
01-01-1994	$3500	3.00

Graph and Chart courtesy of workzone.com

Charts are popular because they turn otherwise large, tedious, reports into visual friendly charts.

Excel provides you everything you need to create wonderful charts. Using this powerful software, you can create a chart or graph without having to export anything using other tools.

While graphs and charts are used interchangeably and make data visualization simple and effective, they are technically two different and separate items and are also independent of each other.

How to Create Charts

Choose the Type of Chart you Desire

Even before you choose the data range or type that you wish to chart, you need to at least have an idea of the kind of chart you wish to create.

Charts are generally more visually pleasing compared to graphs. A simple pie chart can convey a message to viewers in a very simple yet extremely effective approach.

Basically, the type of data being displayed will often determine the kind of chart that you should use.

In situations where you can use a number of charts, then select the type that enables viewers to best visualize the relationships and patterns that exist between the data values.

Most Popular Types of Charts

Pie Charts

These charts essentially provide a visual display of the percentage of each unit within a series. These charts are best to use in situations where values in a series are being compared as percentages of the whole.

Bar Chart

This type of chart displays the values of a series using horizontal bars or columns. It is quite effective when comparing large volumes of data in a single series and is also great for multiple series.

Column Chart

The column chart makes use of vertical columns to display the values or data of a series within a certain period of time. These column charts are especially important when you need to compare values for a number of series. This chart displays columns on 3 axes which are Z, X, and Y.

Line Chart

A line chart simply displays points that are equally positioned and connected via a line.

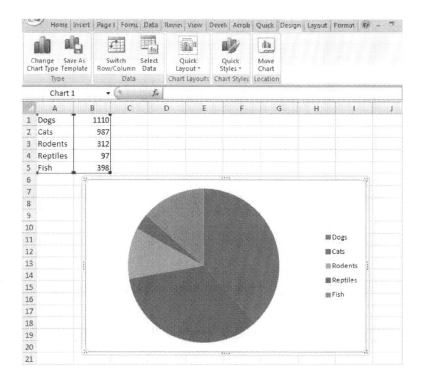

Pie chart in Excel courtesy of Statisticshowto.com

How to Choose Data for your Chart

When you decide to create a chart, you will need to select data from your worksheets.

All you need to do in this case is to identify the cells that have the data you wish to display on a chart. Now, using the cursor, click and drag from the initial to the last cell at the bottom right-hand side of your worksheet.

Remember to include headings. Some data that may be on your spreadsheet, such as a total's column will not feature on the chart.

You can select non-contiguous columns and rows of cells by simply pressing CTRL key and using the mouse to select the specific cells.

A related set of values or data is referred to as a data series. You can have a single or multiple data series. Most charts will let you plot both single and multiple data series.

Creating a Chart on MS Excel

- First, go to Excel ribbon and select insert tab

- Next, choose the chart type from the chart section and click on a preferred sub-type

- The chart will shortly thereafter appear on your worksheet

- You can also create an additional chart on the same worksheet if you need to

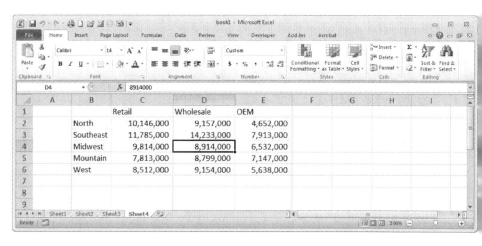

Excel workbook courtesy of k2e.com

Therefore, it is evident that creating a new chart is simply a matter of clicking your cursor in the data range that you wish to showcase.

For instance, you can press F11 after clicking on the data range. This will trigger Excel to pick your preferred chart style and then chart the data range. Use F11 if you want the chart on a different page from the data. On the other hand, use CTRL+F1 if they are to be on the same page.

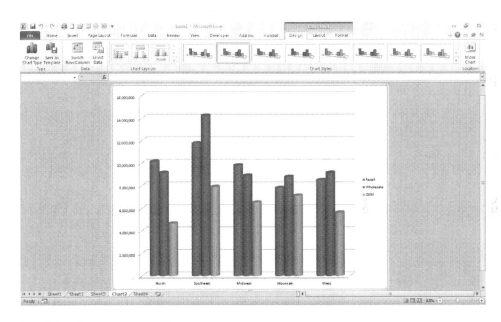

Resulting chart courtesy of k2e.com

You can also delete, resize, and move charts. Here is how to achieve all these;

Deleting a Chart

If you wish to delete a chart in Excel that has just been created, first select excel Undo function.

If the chart is still new, it will be deleted instantly. However, to delete an already existing chart, then you should first highlight the chart in question then click on the delete button, and that's it.

You can alternatively use the Cut function to delete an existing chart.

How to Relocate a Chart

If you need to move a chart to the desired location, then you should first highlight the chart then drag it to the desired destination. This is a pretty easy step.

However, if you wish to move your chart from an existing worksheet to a different worksheet but within the same workbook, then just Right click inside the chart and choose Move Chart.

Thereafter, you will need to choose the destination worksheet. You can also resize the chart, if you want to, by selecting the chart then dragging any of its corners.

Useful Tips for your Excel Charts

- Try as much as possible to keep the chart simple and with no clutter.

- It is a much better idea to have multiple charts than one that is overly cluttered.

- Also, try and have your chart to be as colorful as possible. These are best for online display and visualization.

- For charts that have to be printed, try and use black and grey colors appropriately as these give the best appearance when printed out.

Producing Reports in Excel

Excel allows you to create reports and display a wide variety of data. The reports come with all sorts of visual appeal that will entice the reader to look at the critical data and the information provided therein.

PivotTable is an Excel feature that enables you to summarize and organize data as required. It helps users to compile presentable reports using any kind of data on their workbooks.

Such visual presentations from Excel like graphs and reports are more user-friendly compared to rows and columns. Users can easily assimilate and disseminate information when it is graphically presented.

Excel enables you to create reports that add value to your data. For instance, numbers can be converted into currency, phone numbers, or even zip codes.

Reports provide one of the best ways of bringing your data to life.

✒ How to Create Reports ✒

First, launch Excel and open a new workbook

Then go to the ribbon and click on the "Insert" tab. Now select the "Header and Footer." This icon is in the Text group so enter the preferred name for the report. This will now be the name of your new report.

Go to the Navigation group and choose "Go to Footer" on the Design tab. You can also choose the "Header and Footer Elements" group. This could be options such as "Current Date" or "Page Number."

Now choose one of the data cells and opt for "Click to Add Data" option. Now click "Normal" which is an option in the Workbook Views on View tab. Then enter some data labels in the first columns and rows of your spreadsheet then press the "Tab" so you can save the cell and move on to the next one.

Click on any cell to enter data then save the cell and then proceed to the next one. You can then move on to the next row and repeat the process.

Now identify the data that needs to be grouped together. You can do this by pointing your mouse and locating the cursor at the left side of the cells with the data.

Now choose a number of cells with the relevant data and proper labels. Now click on the tab "Other Charts" to display a list of all available charts.

Click "OK" to save the changes made.

Use PivotTable to Create Reports

PivotTable is an Excel feature that enables you to organize data and present it as a summary yet the data set remains unchanged.

Also, PivotTable enables you to analyze information which would otherwise require additional knowledge and analysis using other features. Here is how to go about it.

How to Create a Report with PivotTable

The report that you will create will only be as great as the data you have, so ensure that your data is accurate and its integrity intact.

Also, ensure that your data has no subtotals, contains no blank columns or rows, and is in a tabulated manner. Ensure that each column of your data has a unique name.

Once all this is confirmed, you can now proceed to create a few reports manually using pen and paper.

This way, you will have a guide to follow even as you proceed with the Excel report. Here is the procedure.

- Select a number of cells within your dataset then click the "insert tab" And choose the PivotTable found in the Tables group. A dialogue box will appear. There you must specify the range for the PivotTable on your worksheet. It could be an existing or new one.

- Once you have chosen the preferred destination worksheet, Excel will display an empty PivotTable frame. As soon as it appears, you can proceed to start pulling in columns. These will be obtained from the "PivotTable Fields (this will show up towards the extreme right of the worksheet). Ensure that data is located in the appropriate section. For instance, values, rows, columns, and so on.

- Your PivotTable frame comes completely empty, so you have to feed it with data. Make sure that you provide the time and date for the necessary fields in the columns, add numerals where they are required for analysis and also descriptive values across the rows.

North Region Unit Sales by City							July 2006
Region	Jan-06	Feb-06	Mar-06	Apr-06	May-06	Jun-06	Jul-06
Actuals							
Seattle	111	653	1,598	3,411	3,972	5,092	5,290
Boise	26,779	27,867	29,153	30,557	33,402	35,400	35,450
Portland	33,078	34,401	37,535	39,916	41,357	45,306	46,671
Spokane	25,417	26,669	28,092	29,020	29,674	30,501	30,838
North Region	199,841	211,053	226,789	242,957	256,605	273,640	277,777
Plan							
Seattle	693	468	790	1,383	2,205	3,180	4,213
Boise	29,525	26,062	27,088	28,269	29,536	30,821	32,166
Portland	32,276	34,708	36,737	38,857	41,066	43,364	45,750
Spokane	30,500	26,644	27,987	29,430	30,994	32,594	34,231
North Region	191,783	203,916	216,524	230,474	246,390	263,378	281,228
Variance							
Seattle	-582	185	808	2,029	1,767	1,912	1,076
Boise	-2,746	1,805	2,064	2,288	3,866	4,578	3,285
Portland	802	-307	798	1,059	291	1,942	921
Spokane	-5,082	25	105	-410	-1,320	-2,093	-3,393
North Region	8,057	7,137	10,265	12,483	10,215	10,261	-3,451

An excel report courtesy of exceluser.com

The main purpose of the PivotTable is to summarize data. These tables can count both text and values. Numbers can be counted by region and other parameters.

Always remember that PivotTable is not dynamic so you always have to refresh if you make any changes to the original data. This way, the changes will reflect on your PivotTable. The process of creating a table is also very simple.

- Pick one of the cells in your dataset

- Go to the ribbon and choose the Insert tab

- Then get to the Tables group and choose Table

- Choose the header row for your data set

- Now click OK so that the selected dataset is converted into a table

You can create a PivotTable simply by choosing the Insert tab found on the Excel ribbon or opting for Summarize with PivotTable.

This is only if you are using a table. It is advisable to use tables as a source of data because it will save you plenty of valuable time and the problem of remembering to update the PivotTable on a regular basis.

However, sources can vary, and your regular rows and columns can also provide the data.

PivotTables are definitely an important option of professionally presenting data and results accurately. They can be used to present sales figures, the performance of a stock, and so much more. They are excellent for providing a suitable summary.

Important Points to Note

- You should consider creating your own spreadsheet first and then create some reports and tables, just to confirm if you can apply some of these useful techniques.

- Any data that you provide which is too wide to fit in a column will spill over into adjacent cells as long as they are blank.

- You should ensure that you create a backup to any live spreadsheets before making any changes. Only after saving and having a backup should you then make any changes you deem essential.

Chapter 10

✎Excel Templates & Themes ✎

An Introduction to Excel Templates

Microsoft Excel allows you to create or use templates in your Excel workbooks. You can either create one for yourself or use one that has been created by others.

Even after creating your own templates, you can make adjustments and a few tweaks if you deem them necessary to improve the overall look of your workbook.

These templates are useful because they enable you to create attractive and consistent documents that are presentable and will impress whoever gets to read them. Your workmates, colleagues, clients, and even bosses will be impressed when they receive a report that you prepared if it comes with a suitable template.

Templates come in handy for documents that are regularly used. These include invoices, budget planners, calendars, dashboards, and inventories among many others.

It is so much easier and very convenient to pick up a spreadsheet report that is aptly presented yet contains all the useful information that you need.

✒ What is an Excel Template ✒

An Excel template is simply a pre-designed worksheet or workbook in which most of the layout and outline has already been done.

This saves you a lot of time and prevents having to do all the work. There are plenty of free Excel templates that you can find online and use for your very own work.

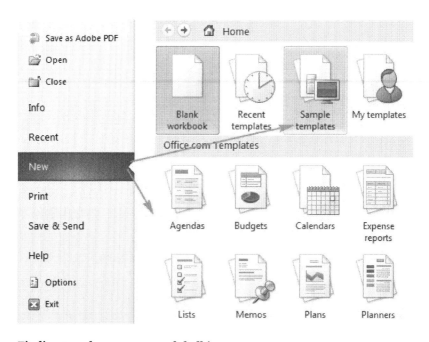

Finding templates courtesy of abelbits.com

How to Create Workbooks from an Excel Template

If you choose to work with an Excel workbook, then you can easily and conveniently create a workbook that is based on an existing Excel workbook.

If you can find the right template, then it will help you a lot when it comes to matters of style, formulas, and plenty of other features.

Here are the steps you should follow if you are to create a new workbook that is based on a current template.

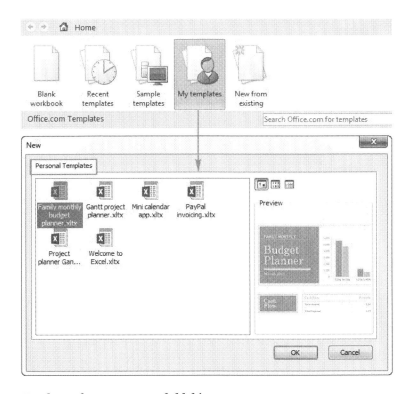

Excel templates courtesy of ablebits.com

- First, open a new workbook. Then click **new** from the "File" tab. You will then see plenty of templates that you can choose and use for free. You will get a chance to select from a couple of Excel templates which are already installed on your computer or download some that you can also select and use.

- Take some time and preview a couple of these templates. If you see one that you like and wish to use or work with, then simply click "Create" and it will be downloaded. During the preview, you will know about the template's creator, the name, and other useful details. Now if you choose a template such as the Mini Calendar, then click "Create" and download it.

- Once you click and download your preferred template, it will be ready for use, and you can use it to create a new workbook.

- Sometimes you may need to use a specific template for a particular purpose. If that is the case, then you will have to browse through an entire list or catalog of templates.

Please note that when you search for appropriate or suitable templates to use, you will have access to a wide variety to choose from. MS Excel has a large variety available at the MS Office store. However, not all are from Microsoft, and some are privately designed by third-party suppliers.

Make your Own Excel Template

With time, you are likely to find that you use one or more Excel templates more than others. You may also wish to have your very own template that is customized according to your wishes and desires.

Fortunately, Excel allows and enables you to do this. If you invest just a little of your time and effort, you can have a practical, beautiful, and presentable template that you can use any time you wish.

As a matter of fact, Excel permits the creation of two different kinds of templates.

These are the Sheet.xltx and Book.xltx. Basically, you can choose between an Excel Workbook template and Excel Worksheet template.

The Workbook template typically comes with a number of sheets with default text such as row and column labels, headers, and so on. You can then add any macros, formulas, and functions. You can also apply any kinds of formatting and styles you desire so that you have new workbooks designed according to this template.

Download Excel Templates

If you wish, you can download Excel templates directly to your device. One of the best sources of templates is definitely www.office.com. Here you will be able to identify and download a whole lot of templates.

There are plenty of free and specific ones including calendars, project management templates, invoices, budget templates, and many more. If you need something specific, then you may want to search on other websites.

The good news is that you can search via template categories which makes things much easier. Once you find one that you like, then you can easily download it directly onto your computer.

If you download the templates from third-party websites, then ensure that you do so only from trusted sites.

Excel Themes

Excel themes are ideally a bunch of shapes, font styles, and default colors. Most of these are built into Excel and can be accessed via the Page Layout Menu.

Ideally, document themes from Excel ensure that you can easily manage graphic formatting effects, fonts, and colors on your workbooks and worksheets.

You can update these features any time you want to. In fact, you can make changes to your entire Excel theme if you wish to.

If you decide to make changes to the general appearance, colors, or fonts in your worksheets and workbook, simply switch themes and see how this works out for you.

You can use one or more of the themes provided or customize a theme that you like or prefer. And the best part about themes is that if you like one, then you can not only customize it but also make it your default theme.

By visiting your Excel's Page Layout menu, you will be able to view all the themes available. Browsing through them is pretty easy. Simply hover your mouse over the themes, and each will be highlighted. You will then be able to view its layout, colors, and fonts.

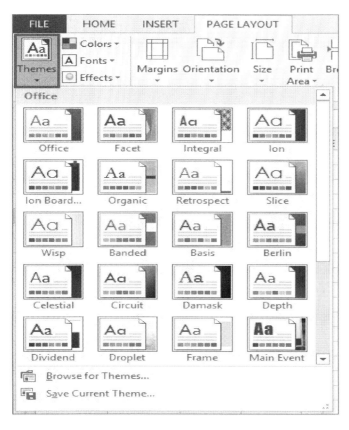

Excel themes courtesy of support.office.com

If you wish to change and customize the effects, fonts, colors, and so on, simply click on the theme and begin from here.

Just go the Page Layout and choose colors. You will then be able to pick a preferred color from here. Most of the time the first set of colors is the default used by the particular theme. You are also able to skip the sets of colors and customize colors as you wish.

If you wish to keep any changes that you make, then always ensure that you save them. This way, your customized or preferred themes will take precedence.

Chapter 11

⟲ Useful EXCEL Tips ⟲

While Excel is still widely used around the world, most of its features remain largely unused and poorly understood. Even those who use it regularly do not understand how to perform simple operations such as formatting.

Fortunately, it is possible to improve your Excel skills and ensure that you can effectively use and benefit from this amazing spreadsheet software.

We will examine some of the tips that will ensure you can use Excel effectively from now on.

Learn how to use Conditional Formatting

It is important to be able to figure out data collected on an Excel worksheet.

Conditional formatting helps portray the data and present a clear image and any existing patterns.

Many users consider conditional formatting as the single most important feature that you and every excel user should learn.

Make use of PivotTables

PivotTables are absolutely useful when you need to sort out data onto a single spreadsheet.

PivotTables can count, sort, and work out the average or total amount of data stored on a worksheet. The outcome will be displayed in a table known as a PivotTable.

Copy and Paste between cells

Another very common activity on Excel spreadsheets is copying data from one cell and then pasting it onto another.

However, errors do occur, and the process can be tedious if there is a lot of work involved. It is much easier to copy cell contents and transfer only the values, minus the formatting, to your worksheet.

The easiest way to do this is to copy using CTRL C and then transfer the values using ALT ESV.

Add a Number of Rows

There are numerous times when adding rows to your data is essential. It is also among the most common activities on Excel. Fortunately, you can use an effective shortcut to cut the time and reduce errors and inaccuracies.

Basically, you only have to Right-click to add a couple of rows. You can choose as many columns and rows as you wish then click Right-click and proceed to add them.

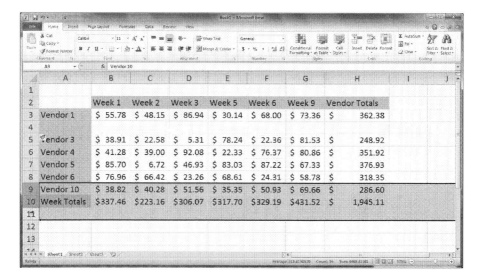

Add multiple rows courtesy of learn filtered.com

Print Optimization

It is important to learn how to optimize printing in MS Excel.

Printing Excel spreadsheets can be challenging, and most people experience problems trying. However, it is possible to print exactly what you want to.

What you need to learn to do is check and confirm accuracy using features such as print selection, print preview, printing headers, adjust margins and a couple of others. If you can learn how to use these simple features, then you will never experience any challenges when printing Excel documents.

Use Filters

Using filters enables you to explore data fast, easy, and effectively.

The process of filtering some data will hide a lot that is of no use at all.

For instance, if you are looking for yellow roses within your data, this function can hide everything else and let you see only that which you wish to view.

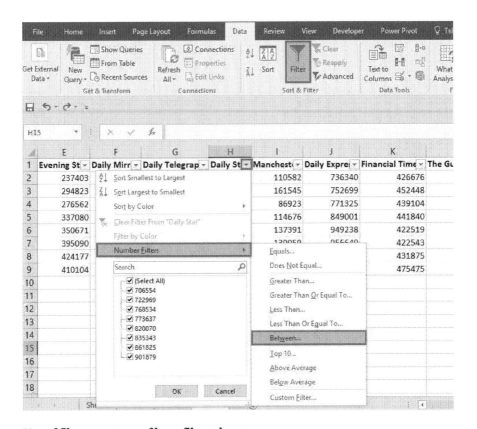

Use of filters courtesy of learnfiltered.com

Conclusion

I hope this book was able to help you learn the essentials of Excel 2016 and inspire you to use this application to achieve your goals.

The next step is to master as many of these tips and techniques to improve your skills with this extremely popular spreadsheet software. Excel is a very powerful program, but sadly, not many of us know how to use its complete feature set.

By learning more about Excel, you will not only be more proficient but also able to produce better reports that showcase your skills and present you as a true professional who works smart and delivers excellent reports.

I wish you the very best of luck!

Preview of Python For Beginners

✎ Python Variables and Operators ✎

$\mathcal{A}$s with any programming language, in Python it is critical to understand variables and the operators used to manipulate them.

Variable usage in Python is much easier than in more structured languages such as C/C++. Even so, variables and their operators still function on a basic set of rules which cannot be ignored. If you attempt to do something outside the rules, an exception will be thrown.

In this chapter we will go over some of those rules for defining variables, variable typing, variable scope, and variable operations.

Let's start off with one important broad Python variable concept that might take a little thinking to wrap your head around.

Python classes all variables as objects which are either mutable or immutable.

On the surface you would think that mutable means it can change and immutable means it cannot change. But what good is a variable that cannot change?

In fact, one would think that an immutable object is simply a constant.

However, integers, floats, strings and others in python are all considered immutable even though their values can in fact be changed.

For example if we went to the shell in IDLE and entered the following:

```
>>>X=10
>>X+=10
>>print(X)
```

we would get X=20, as expected.

So, how is that immutable?

It is all in the magic behind the scenes!

What the interpreter actually does is create an object X in memory. When the operation is performed to add 10 to X, a new object is created in memory containing 20 and X is pointed to that.

The old value of 10 is no longer referenced and is discarded. This may seem like a distinction without a difference until you combine this with the fact that Python is managing memory on the fly as the script runs (unlike C/C++ where you as the programmer manage memory).

If you are doing a lot of functions, like string concatenation, that use immutable objects then you are in fact doing memory intensive operations.

To make your programs as efficient as possible, many of those operations can be done with mutable objects.

Doing so will require a good understanding of those objects and some planning or creative thinking to make them useful for the task.

Immutable Objects: Boolean, Integer, Float, Complex, Tuple, String, Frozenset

Mutable Objects: List, Set, Dictionary, Bytearray

Things start to get even stranger when you consider that some immutable objects can contain mutable objects and vice versa.

For example, a **tuple** can contain both a string (immutable) and a List (mutable).

What the tuple is really storing is a reference in memory to the included object.

Since immutable objects change memory location when altered the reference in the tuple will always point to the original unaltered version.

Lists on the other hand are mutable and their reference in the tuple will always point to its current form.

If a function changes the contents of a list, that change appears when the list is pulled from the tuple. If a function changes a string in a tuple, the original string with still be present in the tuple. Here is an example:

```
>>> a=list('Car')    # a is a list
>>> b='Apple' # b is a string
>>> c=(a,b)    # c is a tuple with a & b
>>> print(c)
(['C', 'a', 'r'], 'Apple')
```

Now if we go back and change the first character in the list a (which is mutable) to a 'B' and then print the tuple c again you will see that the data in c (which referenced a) has changed.

The change reflects the change we made to a.

```
>>> a[0]='B'
>>> print(c)
(['B', 'a', 'r'], 'Apple')
```

If we change the value of the string b (which is immutable) and reprint the tuple c, the original value if b is still shown.

```
>>> b='Orange'
>>> print(c)
(['B', 'a', 'r'], 'Apple')
```

In highly structured languages like C/C++, variables have to be declared, typed and sized.

Failure to do so will result in compilation errors and can lead to a great deal of frustration. This is not the case with Python.

*I*f you are interested in learning Python, please do check out

PYTHON For Beginners: A Smarter and Faster Way to Learn Python

https://www.amazon.com/dp/B07CWQ4DQ5

Made in the USA
Middletown, DE
12 January 2019